Nature Starts

Whose BABY Is This?

by Julie Murphy

CAPSTONE PRESS
a capstone imprint

A+ Books are published by Capstone Press,
1710 Roe Crest Drive, North Mankato, Minnesota 56003.
www.capstonepub.com

 Books published by Capstone Press are manufactured with paper
containing at least 10 percent post-consumer waste.

Library of Congress Cataloging-in-Publication Data
Murphy, Julie, 1965–
  Whose baby is this? / by Julie Murphy.
    p. cm.—(A+ Books. Nature starts)
  Includes bibliographical references.
  Summary: "Simple text and full-color photos ask multiple-choice questions about which
adults baby animals grow up to be"—Provided by publisher.
  ISBN 978-1-4296-7553-6 (library binding) – ISBN 978-1-4296-7853-7 (paperback)
  1. Animals—Infancy—Juvenile literature. I. Title. II. Series.
QL763.M87 2012
591.3'92—dc23
                                                              2011027265

Credits

Katy Kudela, editor; Juliette Peters, designer; Marcie Spence and Svetlana Zhurkin,
    media researchers; Laura Manthe, production specialist

A special thanks to Debbie Folkerts, PhD, Department of Biological Sciences,
    Auburn University, Alabama, for her time and expertise on this project.

Photo Credits

Alamy: BristolK, cover (left), 8, China Span/Keren Su, 14; Ardea: Steve Downer, 12, Tom and Pat Leeson,
13 (top left); Corbis: Visuals Unlimited/Dr. John D. Cunningham, 26, Visuals Unlimited/Gary Meszaros, 22;
Dreamstime: Aleksandr Bondarchiuk, 11 (bottom right), Arie v.d. Wolde, 13 (bottom right), Dmitry Kalinovsky,
6, Jeff Grabert, 16; Shutterstock: alslutsky, 23 (top left), Alta Oosthuizen, 27 (bottom left), Anna Kucherova,
3, Arnold van Wijk, 19 (bottom left), Arto Hakola, 25 (bottom left), Bruce MacQueen, 30, Cathy Keifer, 11
(bottom left), 23 (bottom right), Cigdem Sean Cooper, 27 (top right), 29 (bottom right), CLFProductions, 15
(bottom left), Cristian Mihai, 17 (bottom left), D. Kucharski & K. Kucharska, 24, Dan Rodney, 15 (top right),
Dennis Donohue, 7 (bottom left), Fong Kam Yee, 25 (bottom right), Gentoo Multimedia, 18, Hung Chung
Chih, 15 (bottom right), 28 (bottom right), Igor Borodin, 4–5, Ivan Kuzmin, 23 (top right), Jason Mintzer, 21
(bottom right), Jason Patrick Ross, 20, John Lindsay-Smith, 7 (bottom right), Joyce Mar, cover (middle right),
9 (top right), Judy Kennamer, cover (top right), 9 (top left), Kris Holland, 25 (top right), L.L. Masseth, 15
(top left), Lavigne Herve, 27 (top left), Leighton Photography & Imaging, 17 (top right), 29 (top left), Lilyana
Vynogradova, cover (bottom left), 9 (bottom left), 28 (top right), Mark Bridger, 17 (bottom right), Matthew W.
Keefe, 5, Maynard Case, 21 (top right), Michael Leggero, 19 (top left), mikeledray, 1, 10, Nancy Bauer, cover
(middle right), 9 (bottom right), Rafael Ramirez Lee, 13 (bottom left), 28 (bottom middle), Ronnie Howard,
7 (top left), Rudy Umans, 21 (top left), 29 (top right), Ryan M. Bolton, 23 (bottom left), 29 (bottom left),
Sbolotova, 7 (top right), 28 (top left), Sergei Chumakov, 11 (top left), 28 (bottom left), Sergey Uryadnikov, 21
(bottom left), Susan Flashman, 13 (top right), Vinicius Tupinamba, 17 (top left), visceralimage, 19 (top right),
William Ju, 19 (bottom right), 29 (top middle), worldswildlifewonders, 11 (top right), Yai, 27 (bottom right),
Yellowj, 25 (top left), 29 (bottom middle)

Note to Parents, Teachers, and Librarians

This Nature Starts book uses full color photographs and a nonfiction format to introduce the
concept of animal life cycles. *Whose Baby Is This?* is designed to be read aloud to a pre-reader
or to be read independently by an early reader. Photographs help listeners and early readers
understand the text and concepts discussed. The book encourages further learning by including
the following sections: Glossary, Read More, and Internet Sites. Early readers may need assistance
using these features.

Printed in the United States of America in North Mankato, Minnesota.
102011   006405CGS12

BABIES IN THE WILD

Big and small, short or tall, all animals start out as babies. Some babies look like small copies of their parents. Others look nothing like their parents.

Many babies are born helpless. They need their parents to keep them safe. But some babies take off on their own right from the start. These babies never meet their parents.

It's a big world out there! Animal babies have a lot to learn. Babies that stay safe grow into adults. Then they may have babies of their own.

Can you guess each animal's baby?

Keep reading and make your best guess! You can find the correct answers on pages 28 and 29.

At first this baby needs its mother's help to stay warm. But within weeks, this baby is ready to play. Some people share their homes with this animal. They treat it like one of the family.

WHOSE BABY IS THIS?

FOX

DOG

WOLF

HYENA

Hint ! This animal is the world's oldest pet.
People call it "man's best friend."

This baby's gray and white feathers make it look nothing like its bright pink parents. As the chick grows, it eats millions of tiny, pink shrimp. Eating shrimp helps turn this bird's feathers pink.

WHOSE BABY IS THIS?

PURPLE FINCH

PINK COCKATOO

FLAMINGO

SPOONBILL

Hint!

This bird catches food with its head upside down. Its beak digs in the mud and strains out dirt and water. Gulp! The bird swallows the food left behind.

In the hollow of a rain forest tree, a mother has guarded her eggs and kept them warm. Yellow, red, or brown babies soon hatch from the eggs. In a year or two, these babies will be as green as the trees they live in.

WHOSE BABY IS THIS?

GREEN TREE PYTHON

GREEN TREE FROG

CHAMELEON

GREEN MAMBA

 Hint!

This animal has a tail with a skinny tip. When the tip wriggles, it looks like a worm. Any curious animals that come too close could end up as lunch!

Only the size of a jellybean at birth, this joey snuggles in its mother's pouch. It drinks her milk and grows. When it leaves its mother's pouch, this joey will not crawl, walk, or run. It will jump using its strong back legs.

WHOSE BABY IS THIS?

OPOSSUM

TASMANIAN DEVIL

KANGAROO

KANGAROO MOUSE

Hint!

This joey makes its home in Australia.
It hops around deserts and grasslands.

It's hard to imagine this sleeping baby will grow into a giant. To grow big and strong, this cub will eat lots of bamboo. A bone in its front paws acts like a thumb to grip bamboo.

WHOSE BABY IS THIS?

RACCOON

KOALA

GRIZZLY BEAR

GIANT PANDA

Hint  This is one of the world's most threatened animals. It lives in the forests of China.

This baby munches on leaves. But no one nibbles on this baby. It looks like a blob of bird poop! This creepy crawly later turns green and then becomes a pupa. Inside the pupa's changing room, it becomes an adult.

WHOSE BABY IS THIS?

EARTHWORM

TIGER SWALLOWTAIL BUTTERFLY

MOTH

LADYBUG

 Hint!

This animal gets part of its name from the yellow and black pattern on its wings.

In the world's coldest place, this baby began inside an egg. Snug and warm, the egg sat on its father's feet. Now soft feathers keep this chick warm. Soon this chick will grow black and white waterproof feathers.

WHOSE BABY IS THIS?

DOVE

BALD EAGLE

PUFFIN

EMPEROR PENGUIN

 Hint!

This bird is the largest of its kind. It stands nearly 4 feet (1.2 meters) tall.

This small, stripy baby has sharp teeth, hard scales, and strong jaws. When it grows up, this cold-blooded creature will eat almost anything. Right now, many animals hunt it. This baby usually stays close to its mother.

WHOSE BABY IS THIS?

AMERICAN ALLIGATOR

BEARDED DRAGON

KOMODO DRAGON

GILA MONSTER

 Hint! This kind of animal has been on Earth for millions of years. It lived with the dinosaurs!

This baby swims and has gills like a fish. Its parents look like shiny, wet lizards. But this baby is not a fish or a lizard! Adults live in leaves near ponds. They breathe with their lungs and skin.

WHOSE BABY IS THIS?

CHAMELEON

TOAD

SALAMANDER

GECKO

Hint! Bright spots make this animal stand out. But this animal knows how to stay safe. It hunts only at night.

23

This baby is an insect hunter. Soon it will stop eating. It will shed its skin and become a pupa. In about a week's time, it will become an adult. Adults have shiny, bright bodies with black dots on their backs.

WHOSE BABY IS THIS?

LADYBUG

FROG

BUTTERFLY

SPIDER

 Hint! Farmers like this animal. It eats the insects that chomp on crops in farm fields.

These babies hatched and floated around for months in the sea. They have already changed shape a few times. But they still don't look like their parents. Their parents have bumpy skin, two stomachs, and five arms!

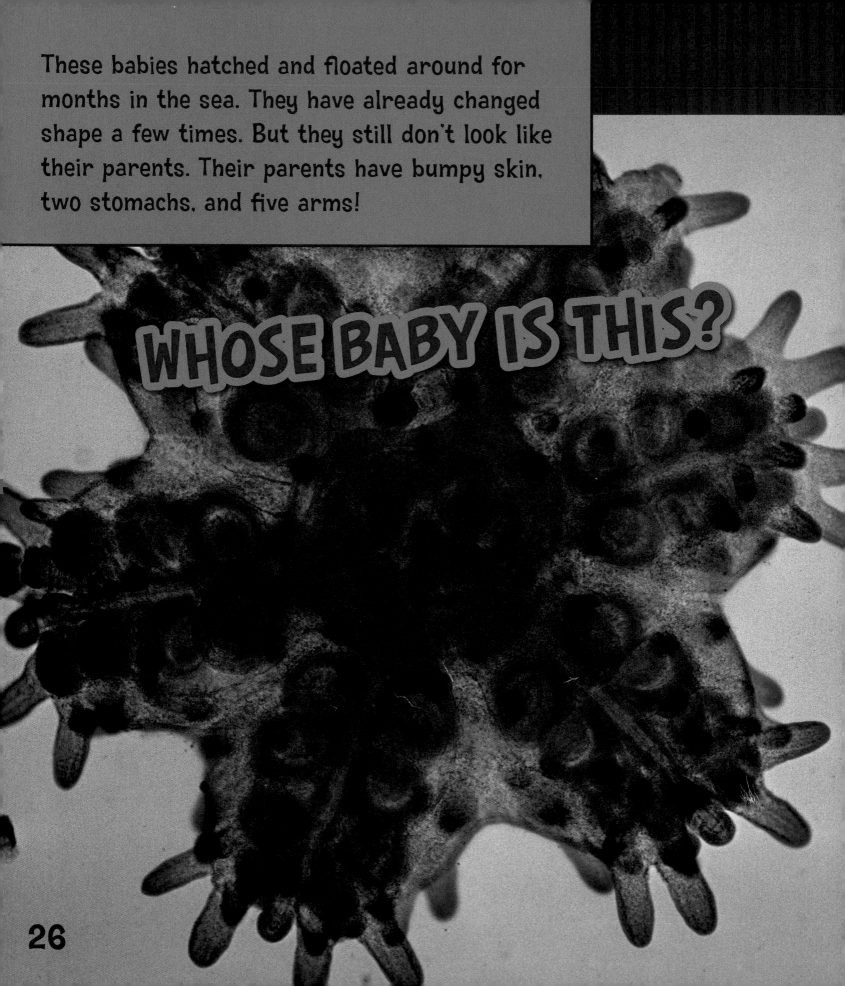

WHOSE BABY IS THIS?

OCTOPUS

SEA STAR

SEA ANEMONE

CRAB

Hint! This animal is not shiny, but it is named after something that twinkles.

Guess Who?

Did you guess the parents of these babies? Check out the answer key to find out if you were correct.

PAGES 6-7

This pup came from a litter of Siberian huskies. **DOGS** are popular pets. At least one in every three U.S. households has a pet dog.

PAGES 8-9

This baby's pink parents are **FLAMINGOS**. A mother flamingo feeds her chick for about two months. Then the chick's beak is big enough to catch its own food.

PAGES 10-11

Baby **GREEN TREE PYTHONS** hide near the ground. They move into the leafy canopy when their skin turns green.

PAGES 12-13

Can you believe that this joey is a **RED KANGAROO**? It starts out tiny, but it grows a lot. Adults can grow over 5 feet (1.5 meters) tall. The red kangaroo is the world's largest marsupial.

PAGES 14-15

The mother of this tiny baby is a **GIANT PANDA**. The cub stays with its mom for about two years.

28

Hatching from an egg, this baby's caterpillar stage doesn't last long. This baby will turn into a **TIGER SWALLOWTAIL BUTTERFLY**.

This fluffy chick's father is an **EMPEROR PENGUIN**. Unlike most penguins, emperor penguins do not build nests. The males keep the eggs warm and safe on their feet.

When this baby grows up, it will be a strong **AMERICAN ALLIGATOR**. Males grow to be over 15 feet (4.6 meters) long. That's as long as a car!

The parents of this tadpole are **SPOTTED SALAMANDERS**. These animals are small. But their poisonous skin keeps them safe from predators.

A **LADYBUG** begins its life as an egg. It goes through several stages of growth before it becomes an adult. New adults have soft, pink bodies. Their shells harden into bright red or orange.

This baby's mother is a **SEA STAR**. There are about 2,000 kinds of sea stars. These sea creatures live in all of the world's oceans.

Animal babies may be cute. But these animals have a lot of growing to do. They can be easily hurt. If you find a baby animal in the wild, remember not to get too close. You might scare the baby or its parents, which may be nearby.

Glossary

bamboo—a grass with a hard, hollow stem

beak—the hard front part of the mouth of birds

canopy—the upper layer of the rain forest formed
   by treetops

cold-blooded—having a body temperature that changes with
   the surrounding temperature

gill—a frilly body part on the side of fish, salamanders, and
   other underwater animals; a gill is used for breathing

hatch—to break out of an egg

joey—a young marsupial

marsupial—an animal that carries its young in a pouch

poisonous—able to harm or kill with poison or venom

predator—an animal that hunts other animals for food

pupa—a hard casing with an insect inside; the insect is
   changing from a larva to an adult

Read More

Bredeson, Carmen. *Baby Animals of the World.* Berkeley Heights, N.J.: Enslow Elementary, 2011.

Lundgren, Julie K. *Who Do I Look Like?: A Book about Animal Babies.* My Science Library. Vero Beach, Fla.: Rourke, 2012.

Wilson, Hannah. *Baby Animals.* I Wonder Why. New York: Kingfisher, 2008.

Internet Sites

FactHound offers a safe, fun way to find Internet sites related to this book. All of the sites on FactHound have been researched by our staff.

Here's all you do:

Visit *www.facthound.com*

Type in this code: 9781429675536

 **Super-cool stuff!** Check out projects, games and lots more at www.capstonekids.com